C++

Beginner to Pro Guide

By

Timothy Short

Table of Contents

Introduction

Congratulations on choosing *C++: Beginner to Pro Guide* and thank you for doing so.

The following chapters will discuss the many concepts of C++ and get you on the path to becoming a master of the language. We're going to cover many, many facets of the language, and by the end, you're going to feel very comfortable programming in it.

There are plenty of books on this subject on the market, thanks again for choosing this one! Every effort was made to ensure it is full of as much useful and practical information as possible to give you an amazing learning experience, please enjoy!

Chapter 1: Introduction

C++ is a monolith. It's one of the most widely used programming languages of all time. Though in modernity, it has slightly fallen to the wayside in popular programming due to the prevalence of scripting languages such as Python, Ruby, and Perl, and less esoteric and more natural languages such as Java and C#, C++ is still one of the seminal languages for low-level programming. Any time you've got to do something that requires direct access to the hardware and fast, efficient execution, you should consider C++ as your primary option.

Additionally, since it's so ubiquitous, C++ is an essential language to learn because, as a programmer, you very well could end up maintaining legacy code written in C++.

In other words, C++ is no question a necessity for anybody wishing to seek a serious career in programming.

On top of that, C++ can be a very useful language for hobbyists, too. Many open-source video games are written partially or completely in C++, such as OpenTTD. Arduino circuits are coded in C/C++, as are Raspberry Pi units.

If for no other reason, you should learn C++ due to the simple fact that it's incredibly powerful. C++ will allow you to do almost anything a language *could* allow you to do, while also being super functional and readable. It bridges the gap between lower-level more esoteric languages like C and higher level languages like Java and Python.

Chapter 2: Getting Set Up / Your First Program

Since this is a beginner's guide, I'm going to give you pretty straightforward instructions to getting set up ASAP so that you can get to work. At the same time, though, I'm going to try to explain exactly what's going into what you're downloading.

Two big components of getting started with C++ for a beginner are an IDE and a compiler. An IDE, or **integrated development environment**, is an environment in which you write code which allows you to run and debug your program as well as perform other functions depending on which IDE you use. A **compiler** is what translates what you write into code that the machine can read and understand. Often, the IDE will come bundled with a compiler. It's not absolutely necessary that you have an IDE - you theoretically can write the code in a text editor, save as .cpp, and then compile. However, I don't recommend this, especially not as a beginner to C++ and potentially programming in general.

For this book, I recommend that you get an IDE called CodeBlocks. It can be found at codeblocks.org. You go to the *downloads* page and then click the link titled "download the binary release". If you're running Windows, download the file named "codeblocks-[VERSION]mingw-setup.exe". If you're running Linux, just select the version appropriate for your distribution.

Once you have CodeBlocks installed, you're going to launch it. After launching it, you're going to most likely have a first-time dialog that asks which compiler you'd like to use, with MinGW/GCC selected by default. Just press "ok".

Once you're on to the actual software, you're going to click "file" on the taskbar, then hover over "new >", then select "empty file".

In this file, type the following. It doesn't make much sense yet, but it will.

```cpp
#include <iostream>

using namespace std;

int main() {
    cout << "Hello world\n";
    return 0;
}
```

After typing this, look just below the taskbar on the icon bar for a set of icons. They should be a gear, a play button, and a gear WITH a play button. These are build, run, and build + run. C++ has to be compiled before it's ran. The build option does this. Run, of course, executes the program. Build + run does both.

Click build + run, and watch what happens.

Voila! Your very first C++ program. Now either go to Edit > Save, or press Control+S. Save your file as "first.cpp", and observe what happens to the text.

It comes to life in vibrant colors! This is thanks to the IDE. It's called **syntax highlighting**, which means the IDE is helping you dissect your program into its individual parts.

So there it is: your coding environment, alongside your very first program. In the next chapter, we're going to be exploring something called variables and how you can use them in your program, as well as basic input.

Chapter 3: Variables, Input, and C++ math

This chapter is going to set you up for the rest of your C++ adventure. Programs constantly are using and manipulating data. That's the sole reason they even exist. **Variables** are pieces of data within your program that can be manipulated.

C++ is handy at giving you different ways to interpret this data. There are different forms of data storage, called **data types**.

These data types include:
int - for whole numbers from -2147483648 to 2147483647
float - for floating point numbers, i.e. decimals
double - for double floating point numbers
char - for ASCII characters
bool - used for true/false values

And there are variations of these, which gives you greater control over their ranges.

unsigned int - for unsigned integers (integers which are not negative), has twice the positive range of a normal int (from 0 to 4294967295)
short int - an int from -32768 to 32768. Takes up less bit space than a normal int.

There's one more type that doesn't seem especially important right now but will definitely have applications where it's incredibly important. This is called a *constant*. To declare a constant, you put *const* before the data type of whatever variable you're declaring.

Constants have to have their value given to them when they're declared, and afterward that value is not allowed to change. Full stop.

What we're going to do now is open CodeBlocks and go to File > New... > Project. From the available options, click "Console Application". Make it a C++ project and name it Chapter3. Use the default compiler options.

On your sidebar, expand Chapter3, then expand Sources, then double-click main.cpp. Delete everything in the file, because you're going to learn by practice.

Type the following:

```
#include <iostream>

using namespace std;

int main() {
    int apples = 3; // declare variable "apples",
give it a value

    cout << "I have " << apples << " apples!\n";
// print
    return 0;
}
```

Then build and run.
You should see the console say "I have 3 apples!". If so, fantastic, you did it right.

Short little aside, the double-slash is a comment. There are two kinds of comments.

There are single line comments, as such:

```
// this is a comment
```

These can be added anywhere within the code. It makes the compiler ignore everything which comes afterward on that line of code.

There are also multi-line comments, like this:

```
/* this is
      a multi-line
comment */
```

These are surrounded, as you can see, by /* and */. If you start these, you must terminate them, or else your compiler will think everything after /* is a comment!

So, as you can tell by the comments, what we did here was declared a variable named *apples*, which was an integer (int), and give it a value of 3.

Now you need to manipulate it for yourself. Change the value of apples and try to make it say "I have 6 apples."

But what if we wanted to allow the user to tell us how many apples *they* had? Well, this is where it gets to be a bit fun.

Erase your code all over again (sorry!) and type the following:

```
#include <iostream>

using namespace std;

int main() {
    int apples;

    cout << "How many apples do you have?\n";
    cin >> apples;
    cout << "Wow! You have " << apples << " apples!";

    return 0;
}
```

Let me explain what's going on here.

This time, we declared the variable *apples* but didn't give it a value. We could have given it a value, but for the sake of example, I chose not to.

Then we print out a line which asks the user how many apples they have. *cout* is the standard output method and stands for "console out".

Then we allow the user to input data. We type *cin*, meaning "console in", and used the input stream operator (>>) before the variable that we were reading from the user.

After getting that information, we print it back to the user. The way that *cout* works is that it writes to the console whatever comes through the output stream, designated by the output stream operator (<<). When you write something in quotes, it's actually reading it as a string of text which it simply prints to the console. Since *cout* designates an output stream, we can tie things together and print out any string or variable in our program.

But what if we wanted to know about more than just apples? What if there were pears? Oranges?

I'm going to show you how I'd do it if I were going to ask not only how many apples someone had, but also how many bananas and lemons.

```
#include <iostream>

using namespace std;

int main() {
        int apples, bananas, lemons;

        cout << "How many apples do you have?\n";
        cin >> apples;
        cout << "Well, how about bananas?\n";
        cin >> bananas;
        cout << "And what about lemons?\n";
        cin >> lemons;
        cout << "Wow! You have " << apples << "
apples, " << bananas << " bananas, and " << lemons << "
lemons!\n" ;

        return 0;
}
```

However, note that just like how you can piece a bunch of variables together through the output stream, you can also get a bunch of data at once through the input stream.

Here's an example of that:

```
#include <iostream>

using namespace std;

int main() {
        int apples, bananas, lemons;

        cout << "First enter how many apples you
have, then bananas, then lemons.\n";
        cin >> apples >> bananas >> lemons;
        cout << "Wow! You have " << apples << "
apples, " << bananas << " bananas, and " << lemons << "
lemons!\n" ;

        return 0;
}
```

In this way, C++ was ingeniously designed to be intuitive right from the get-go.

Another thing you very well may find useful going forward is **enumerators**. These allow you to create a sort of "state" statement. Underneath it all, these are just integer values, but they allow you to do some easy comparisons going forward, which we'll jump into in the next chapter.

An enum would be declared like this:

```
enum fruit { apple, banana, lemon, orange, melon
};

fruit fruitOne = apple;
```

It essentially creates a new type that you can use and compare. There are other structures for doing exactly this that are for more nuanced but this is a great rudimentary way of accomplishing it.

Now it's time to talk about the most crucial part of any programming language: the math. See, computers were built for one purpose: computing. Anything that a computer ever does is resultant of a set of computations that happened somewhere within. When you opened this e-book, it was the result of computations within the system which allowed you to launch the application, click the e-book, have it *register* when you clicked the e-book, turn pages in that book, and so on.

Thus, math is crucially important, especially in a language as low-level as C++. Most of what you do with C++ will involve math.

C++ has several different mathematical operators (which, go figure, will come in handy for operator overloading later on in the book.)

The most basic are the ones you've known since grade school:

+ is for addition,
- is for subtraction,
* is for multiplication,
/ is for division.

Great, that's all really simple. Then there are some more complex operators that I'm going to describe.

Firstly, there's the modulo operator, %. What this operator does is determines the remainder of a given division. For example, 13 % 5 gives you a remainder of 3 because 5 goes into 13 twice and then you've got 3 left. Easy-peasy.

On top of that, there are incremental shorthand operators.

i++ would mean i = i + 1,
i-- would mean i = i - 1.

Then there are self-referential shorthand operators:

i+=5 would mean i = i + 5;
i-=5 would mean i = i - 5;
i*=5 would mean i = i * 5;
i/=5 would mean i = i / 5.

All relatively simple. These are the major mathematical operators in C++.

We're actually in a very sweet spot right now where you know what you're doing enough that I can take a moment to talk about the structure of C++ programs without you being entirely lost.

Everything that happens within C++ takes place within various scopes. You don't know too much about functions yet, but they all have their own scope. Classes have their own scope. The main method has its own scope. Everything takes place within an implicit global scope. This makes it easy enough to think about what functions and processes can use what variables.

There are many preferences when it comes to C++ coding, too, because it's not rigid about the way that you write code. Unlike Python for example, where a certain indentation scheme is forced on you, C++ just lets you go and type as you will with little to no problem at all. That is to say that whitespace isn't an issue.

The system sees:

```
cout<<"hello world\n"<<"how are you
today";

    cout << "hello world\n" << "how are you
today";
```

and

```
cout <<
        "hello world\n"
        <<
        "how are you today"
    ;
```

in the exact same manner. That's not to say there aren't conventions; there are. But this does allow you a certain degree of personal expression.

Along the same vein, there is no right or wrong way to name a variable (aside from a few certain *very* wrong ways that won't compile.) As long as your code compiles, you're fine. Try to make it readable, but for all intents and purposes, there's no difference between int NumberOfApples, int numberOfApples, and int number_of_apples except for which specific internet community you might anger by using one way or another.

Similarly, brace style. There are two main forms. I personally use this way:

```
int main() {
    // code here
}
```

because I started programming with Java and it stuck. However, many people also use

```
int main()
{
    // code here
}
```

Again, as long as your code compiles and is readable, you generally are in the clear.

C++ is a relatively intuitive language if you've got an engineering mindset, so you shouldn't have too much trouble catching onto what works and what doesn't. That said, there will be times where you'll be pulling your hair out over a compiler error and, God bless it, your compiler sends you the most cryptic description you could ever imagine. In these cases, there are online communities such as StackOverflow where you can ask questions regarding proper code, as well as how to fix your existent code.

Chapter 4: Conditions and Loops

Now we're going to talk about a few things that will make you program far more logical: logic. Loops and conditions start to utilize math within your program to give different outcomes.

Just like last time, we're going to start this out by creating a new project. Call it Chapter4, and then delete the content of main.cpp.

The first thing we're going to look at is conditions. What conditions do is read a statement or set of statements and determine if it's true or not, and then act accordingly to the code contained therein.

These comparisons are completed using something called *comparison operators*. The comparison operators in C++ are as follows:

== - equal to
!= - not equal to
< - less than
<= - less than or equal to
> - greater than
>= - greater than or equal to

Try to decipher what the following code means:

```
if (card == 4) {
        cout << "I drew a four!\n";
}
```

Got it? This is what's called an *if* statement. It evaluates the statement inside the parentheses, and then if that statement is accurate, it will execute the code within. Now, what about this one?

```
if (card == 2) {
    cout << "I drew a two!\n";
} else if (card == 4) {
    cout << "I drew a four!\n";
} else if (card == 6) {
    cout << "I drew a six!\n";
} else if (card == 8) {
    cout << "I drew an eight!\n";
} else if (card == 10) {
    cout << "I drew a ten!\n";
} else {
    cout << "I didn't draw an even card.\n";
}
```

This introduces the other two kinds of conditional statements: *else if* and *else*. **Else if** follows an if statement and evaluates another condition within the same block of logic. **Else** is an all encompassing statement which you can put after an if statement which will give an absolute command to execute if the if statement's condition isn't true. If you don't include an **else**, don't worry - the code after the if statement will still execute. The way to think about it is this: without an else statement, you're checking solely to see if the condition is accurate; if it's inaccurate, nothing is done. However, if you include an else, you're giving a set of instructions for what to do if the if condition is inaccurate.

But this is blocky. Couldn't we compress this code we just had, to encompass all even cards and odd cards?

Observe the following code.

```
if (card == 2 || card == 4 || card == 6 || card == 8 ||
card == 10) {
    cout << "I drew an even card.";
} else {
    cout << "I drew an odd card.";
}
```

In the first if statement, we use what are called **logical operators**. There are two different types of logical operators.

|| - or
&& - and

The difference between the two is that the or operator checks to see if either expression is true, where the and operator checks to see that both are true.

You can also load multiple expressions into a conditional statement:

```
if (cardNumber == 3 && face == HEARTS ||
cardNumber == 6 && face == SPADES) {
        cout << "You have either a 3 of hearts or a
6 of spades.";
    }
```

The "face" thing is in reference to an enumerator of faces, in reference to the enumerator concept we created earlier. There's a hypothetical enumerator of card faces, as such:

```
enum face { HEARTS, SPADES, DIAMONDS, CLUBS };
```

Another major part of C++ logic is something called a loop. Loops are a way of iterating over a set of data repeatedly. There are a few different ways of completing loops in C++: **while, for,** and **do while**.

While loops are the simplest kind of loop. They're simply made up of a condition during which the code runs, and a set of code which will execute while that condition is true.

In pseudocode:

```
while (run condition) {

        internal code

}
```

If you wanted to create a while loop that counted to five from zero, it'd look like this:

```
int i = 0;

while (i <= 5) {
        cout << i << "\n";
        i++;
}
```

What's happening in this code is that we create an integer, i, with the value 0. We then establish the while loop's run condition: it will run as long as i is less than or equal to 5.

In the loop, we issue a command to print out the current value of the variable i, and then a line break ("\n").

On the next line, we increment i by 1, so when this line is reached, if the integer i was 0, it would become 1. 1 would become 2, and so on.

For loops are especially great for sets of data which need to be iterated incrementally. In pseudocode, here's the way they work.

```
for (starting variable condition; run condition;
starting variable incrementer) {

        internal code

};
```

So if we wanted to implement a *for* loop that counted to five for us, starting at zero, we could do it like this:

```
for (int i = 0; i <= 5; i++) {
        cout << i << "\n";
}
```

To break this down:

```
for (int i = 0;
```

We establish the initial variable by which this loop increments.

```
i <=5;
```

We establish the run condition of this loop. It will run for as long as this condition is met. This is like a miniature while condition.

```
i++) {
```

This is the incremental statement of the for loop. This could be anything mathematical, but for the most part - especially starting out - it will be either incremental addition or incremental subtraction.

The last one, do while is occasionally useful. It executes code once and then continues executing it if a condition is met.

```
char letter;

cout << "Enter the letter B."

do {
     cin >> letter;
} while (letter != 'b');
```

If they enter the letter 'B' on the first time, because for some reason we need to make sure they enter the letter 'B', then fantastic, the code will keep going. If they don't, the program will keep prompting them for input until they do.

While we're on the subject of conditionals and loops, it's important that we discuss one kind of conditional statement that can often be overlooked. It's an important bit of shorthand that can be incredibly useful to a programmer, and can be used in things such as #define statements for function macros (as we'll talk about later.)

This kind of conditional statement is referred to as a ternary operator, and it looks like this.

```
apples == 3 ? "You have three apples!" :
"You don't have three apples..."
```

This makes no sense right now, but let's break it down. A ternary operator has two parts: a condition, and return values.

Everything before the question mark is checked to see if it's true or not. Everything after are the possible return values. If it's true, the value before the colon will be returned. If it's not true, the value after the colon will be returned.

In other words:

condition ? *return* if true : *return* if false

This is great for evaluating statements rather quickly when there are only two results to be returned based on the truthfulness of that statement.

That makes up the overall bulk of the nature of conditional statements and things similar, as well as loops.

Chapter 5: Functions

You may remember from math class at some point where you had to deal with functions, like f(x) = 2x + 5. f(0) would have been 5 (2(0) = 5), f(1) would have been 7 (2(1) + 5), f(2) would have been 9 (2(2) + 5), and so on.

Functions in C++ work similarly.

Functions perform an operation and then often return a value. They don't always have to return a value, however - functions which don't return a value are *void* functions.

First, take a look at this chunk of code. It doesn't have to make sense right now, we're going to go through it. Create a new project called Chapter5 and erase the contents of main.cpp, and type this in.

```
#include <iostream>

using namespace std;

int getArea(int l, int w);

int main()
{
    int length, width;

    cout << "Enter the length, and then enter the
width.\n";
    cin >> length >> width;
    cout << "The area is: " << getArea(length,
width);
    return 0;
}

int getArea(int l, int w) {
    int area = l * w;
    return area;
}
```

So let's break this down line by line.

```
#include <iostream>
```

This includes the essential components for input and output.

```
using namespace std;
```

This denotes that we're using the standard input/output namespace.

```
int getArea(int l, int w);
```

This is where we declare our first function. C++ is procedurally compiled, so you can't just throw functions around willy-nilly. You have to declare them before you write them later, or they have to written entirely before your main function. For the sake of clarity, I prefer initial declaration and then writing the function after my main function, but it's a personal choice. Regardless, we're creating a function here called "getArea". The int before the name denotes that it's going to return an integer value. Likewise, a float getArea(...) would return a float value, a char getChararacter(...) would return a character, and so on.

Within the declaration, we've given two variables, called *arguments*. Much like how in f(x) equations, x was the thing that the equation modified, the argument variables are what our C++ reads in and utilizes.

```
int main()
{
```

This is the start of our main function. In case you haven't figured it out, every program must have a main function. It's the entry point for your code, and the compiler will actively seek it out.

```
int length, width;
```

We declare two variables, length and width.

```
    cout << "Enter the length, and then enter
the width.\n";
    cin >> length >> width;
```

We ask the user to input the length and width, and then accept their input.

```
    cout << "The area is: " << getArea(length,
width);
```

This is where a bit of further explanation is needed. The output stream puts out a value we give it, right? Since functions simply return a value, we can put them straight in the output stream.

Also, since this function returns an integer value, you could also create a new integer and then assign its value as the value of the function, like this:
```
    int area = getArea(length, width);
```

You could then just output:
```
    cout << "The area is: " << area;
```

This is a waste, though, because this variable doesn't need to be created for this program. If you do, however, need to store a variable such as the area of a rectangle, you could do exactly that.

```
        return 0;
    }
```

Simple, every main function must return 0.

```
    int getArea (int l, int w) {
```

This mirrors the function declaration earlier and is where we actually start writing it.

27

```
int area - l * w;
return area;
```

We create a new variable called area, which takes the two arguments from the function header and multiplies them to get its value. We then return that same integer.

We also could have simply written this:
```
return l * w;
```

Both are valid ways of returning this function and will give you an appropriate result.

That's a cursory introduction to functions. They're an absolutely vital way of structuring your program. Programs where everything is only in one function are tedious to read and difficult to maintain. Programs where things are more split up are easier to understand and manage by far.

Chapter 6: Review - Temperature Converter

Now, we're going to tie together a lot of the concepts that we have covered so far by creating something which will convert from Fahrenheit to Celsius or vice versa.

Create a new console application project titled TempConvert, then delete the contents of your main method.

To create this program, we have to consider what all we want it to do.

This, in my mind, is the basic flow of the program.

start program

while the user hasn't prompted to exit:
ask user if fahrenheit to celsius or celsius to fahrenheit
if they input a certain character, let them exit.
if they input F or C, ask them to input the temperature.
convert it, and write the product.

end program

So let's start thinking about how we'd execute this.

We need to start at the beginning, so we'd type

```
#include <iostream>

using namespace std;
```

After that, we're going to need more than one function. Let's make a Fahrenheit conversion function and a Celsius conversion function.

```
float ftoc(float temp);
float ctof(float temp);
```

We gave these the argument "temp" because they're going to take in a temperature that the user enters. After that, we need to create a main function.

```
int main() {
```

With that done, let's think about what variables we need.

First, we need a boolean which will tell us if the loop is active or not. Let's create that.

```
bool run = true;
```

We'll need a character for user input, and we'll also need floating point decimals so that we can accept temperatures. Let's create those.

```
char input;
float temp;
```

Perfect. Now let's create our main program loop:

```
while (run == true) {
```

The reason for making this loop is that somebody may have multiple temperatures to execute, and it would be a pain for them to have to restart the program every single time! It also serves as a way to implement a loop in the context of a program.

After this, we need to tell the user to enter F to convert Fahrenheit to Celsius, C to convert Celsius to Fahrenheit, or E to exit the program. This can be done with a simple *cout* command.

Then we accept their input with a simple *cin* for the character variable. If they enter an E, we need to change the variable "run" to false. This will exit the loop, which is only running *while* run is true.

```
if (input == 'E' || input == 'e') {
        run = false;
}
```

But there's more. We have to parse if it's an F or C as well, so that if statement becomes:

```
if (input == 'E' || input == 'e') {
        return 0;
} else if (input == 'F' || input == 'f') {
        // todo: put code
} else if (input == 'C' || input == 'c') {
        // todo: put code
} else {
        cout << "The character you entered was
invalid, please try again.";
}
```

So now that we've done that, we need to put code in the Fahrenheit and Celsius sections. Under the condition which goes if the input is "F", we need to ask them to input the variable, then print out the converted number. Let's do that. The else if for Fahrenheit should look similar to this:

```
else if (input == 'F' || input == 'f') {
        cout << "Enter the temperature in
Fahrenheit.\n"
        cin >> temp;
        cout << "The temperature in Celsius is: " <<
ftoc(temp);
}
```

Then do the same for Celsius, which is just inverting it.

Afterward, we have to write the logic for those functions. I'll guide you through Fahrenheit to Celsius, but you should do Celsius to Fahrenheit on your own as an exercise.

Let's start like this:

```
float ftoc(float temp) {
      // todo: add code
}
```

The equation for Fahrenheit to Celsius is (F - 32) / 1.8.

We can just implement this in our program in our return value.

```
float ftoc(float temp) {
      return (temp - 32) / 1.8;
}
```

And voilà. As I said, you likely should do the Celsius on your own.

By the end, your program should look somewhat like this:

```cpp
#include <iostream>

using namespace std;

float ftoc(float temp);
float ctof(float temp);

int main()
{
    bool run = true;
    char input;
    float temp;

    while (run == true) {
        cout << "Enter F for Fahr to Celsius, C for
Celsius to Fahr, E to exit.\n";
        cin >> input;

        if (input == 'E' || input == 'e') {
            run = false;
        } else if (input == 'F' || input == 'f') {
            cout << "Enter the temperature in Fahr.\n";
            cin >> temp;
            cout << "The temperature in Celsius is: " <<
ftoc(temp) << ".\n\n\n";
        } else if (input == 'C' || input == 'c') {
            cout << "Enter the temperature in
Celsius.\n";
            cin >> temp;
            cout << "The temperature in Fahr is: " <<
ctof(temp) << ".\n\n\n";
        } else {
            cout << "The character you entered wasn't
valid. Please try again.\n\n\n";
        }
    }

    return 0;
}

float ftoc(float temp) {
    return (temp - 32) / 1.8;
}

float ctof(float temp) {
    return (temp * 1.8) + 32;
}
```

It's a bit messy on this page, but it executes very cleanly and simply. And there you go! There's your first genuine C++ program.

Now it's time to get into some messier concepts like arrays and pointers. After that, we're going to jump into some Standard Template Library things like strings and vectors before finally jumping into classes. There's a long road ahead, but you have enough of a grasp on the basics by now to do pretty simple programs.

Chapter 7: Arrays and Array Algorithms

Now we're getting to one of the more fun concepts. What if you need more than one of a certain object? It's very unwieldy to create variable after variable for the same exact thing.

For example, let's say you had a classroom full of students, and you wanted to keep all of their grades for certain assignments and let's say there were three assignments.

This very well could end up with you having multiple variables as such:

```
int student1grade1, student1grade2,
student1grade3, student2grade1, student2grade2,
student2grade3, ; // and so on...
```

So what if you could simplify them? Well, you can. Let's say your class had 16 students.

With arrays, you could just make the following variables:

```
int assignment1grades[16] = { };
int assignment2grades[16] = { };
int assignment3grades[16] = { };
```

Now you have 16 preallocated variables for each assignment.

You can fill this array with data in two ways. You can either populate them when you declare them:

```
int assignment1grades[16] = {95, 72, 86,
84, 90, 89, (...) };
```

Or you can go in and populate them manually. Arrays start counting at 0, so if you wanted to change the first grade in an array, you would say:

```
assignment1grades[0] = 95;
```

Both are perfectly fine and workable and have their own times that they work best. Choose accordingly.

Now, what if you wanted to list off all of the variables in a populated array? This is where our for loop from earlier comes in handy.

```
for (int i = 0; i < 16; i++) {
        cout << "Grade #" << i + 1 << ": " <<
assignment1grades[i] << "\n";
    }
```

These are called C-style arrays, and are a tad bit deprecated. However, this is crucial knowledge because:

1) They're easier to use and more efficient for beginners than template options, like vectors.
2) They feature heavily in other languages, especially C-style languages e.g. Java and C#.

Since the goal here is to make you a master programmer, let's talk a bit of problem-solving. Let's say we took one of those grades arrays from before, and we wanted to sort it. How could we go about this?

I'm only going to teach you one way, but this manual sort algorithm very well may come in handy, and it's useful for teaching you programming basics. This method of sorting is called bubble sort, and it uses nested loops.

```
int placeholder;
bool swap = true;
while (swap) {
        swap = false;
        for (int i = 1; i < 15; i++) {
            placeholder = 0;
            if (grades[i] < grades[i-1]) {
                placeholder = grades[i];
                grades[i] = grades[i-1];
                grades[i-1] = placeholder;
                swap = true;
            }
        }
    }
```

What this does is create a variable which determines whether there's a swap to be made. For as long as there's still a swap to be made, the variable will be true, and the second loop will iterate all the way through the array, comparing every variable to the one before it ([i] < [i-1]) to see if the current one is smaller than the one before it. If it is, we do a swap of the two variables and set the swap boolean to true so that we don't exit the loop.

Arrays are an excellent starting point to the concept of having more than one of a certain object, and the concept of how C++ manages memory.

There's one more important concept of arrays to cover, which is the idea of multidimensional arrays. Generally, you'll only be using one and two-dimensional arrays, and we've already covered one-dimensional. So what about two-dimensional?

It's a little bit difficult to visualize these but imagine it like this:

```
int arrayName[rows][columns]
```

It's essentially an array of arrays.

For example, array[3][4] would produce an array of three rows and four columns.

You access these by giving a specific index. For the previous example, if there were a 3 by 4 array declared, you'd access them like this:

array[0][0]	[0][1]	[0][2]	[0][3]
array[1][0]	[1][1]	[1][2]	[1][3]
array[2][0]	[2][1]	[2][2]	[2][3]

If you wanted to change the value of the first row, second from the left, you'd type:

```
array[0][1] = value;
```

That's a very simple explanation of multidimensional arrays but should cover it pretty plainly.

Chapter 8: Pointers

This was one of the more difficult concepts for me to grasp, especially starting out. And it's not necessarily easy to grasp, so I'm going to take it slow explaining this because this is actually a huge part of C and C++ programming.

When you create a variable, it's given a specific place in memory. This place in memory is where that variable's value is stored. Any reference to that variable when it's passed to another function is just a copy of that place in memory.

This is fine when you're just working within one function or passing simple arguments to/from, but look at this example.

```
#include <iostream>

using namespace std;

void goWest(int xposition, int yposition);

int main() {
        int xposition = 3, yposition = 3;

        cout << "Your current position is: " <<
xposition << ", " << yposition << "\n";
        cout << "Going west!\n";
        goWest(xposition, yposition);
        cout << "But back in the main function, your
position is: " << xposition << ", " << yposition <<
"\n";
        return 0;
    }

    void goWest(int xposition, int yposition) {
        xposition--;

        cout << "In the goWest function, your
position is: " << xposition << ", " << yposition <<
"\n";
    }
```

Just type that into a file and run it. We're going to be fixing this code anyway. You'll see that what happens is the variable changes in the goWest function, but when we return to the main function, the variable is like it was before. This is because we don't pass the variable directly, but we pass its *value*, and the secondary function makes a copy.

The way to fix this is with pointers. This isn't at all their only use, but it's the simplest way to explain them at this level. Pointers point to a variable's specific address in memory and allow you to access that address and value precisely.

There are two pointer operators:

* - points to a value of an address

& - gets the address of a certain variable

The way that these work is that if you had int x = 3 then &x would point to the place in memory that the variable *x* is stored. Meanwhile, *(&x) would point to the value of x, here 3, and allow you to modify that value directly.

This way, you can bypass the built-in variable protection of C++.

To break it down even more, I'm going to write some code and then translate it into simpler terms.

```
#include <iostream>

using namespace std;

void changeVariable(int * i);

int main() {
    int x = 5;
    cout << "The value of x is: " << x << "\n";
    changeVariable(&x);
    cout << "The value of x is now: " << x << "\n";
}

void changeVariable(int * i) {
    * i = 8;
}
```

So if we were to rewrite this using plain terms:

include iostream

using the standard namespace

declare a function called changeVariable, which takes an argument of a pointer address.

declare the main function

create a variable called x, then print its value.

call the changeVariable function, giving it the address of the variable x,

within the changeVariable function, since we sent it the address as an argument, the argument delimiter "int * i". the "int *" portion takes any given reference address, and since we're sending the address of x, i becomes &x. So the shorthand for what's happening in the function is that it asks for a reference address to give to variable *i - we give it one, the address of x (&x) - and from there, *i points to the value of that address. (5)

change the value pointed to by * i to 8,

output the new value

The only thing that really helps you get this kind of thing is practice. Pointers are easily one of the most difficult concepts to truly comprehend in C/C++, but it's the bread and butter of these languages and is part of what makes them so quick and reliable.

Memory management is the crux of what makes up any good C++ programmer, and knowing your way around pointers is essential to being sufficiently good at programming in C++. Passing around objects, pointers, arrays, templates, all of it gets incredibly frustrating - speaking from experience - *especially* as a newcomer to the language. My principal piece of advice is that you avoid getting discouraged too easily with anything about C++. I want to specify this in the pointers chapter, because it's the most frustrating concept in the entire language for a lot of people.

Chapter 9: Strings

To a certain extent, it feels a little late to be finally getting to strings. But the difference between strings in C++ and higher-level languages like Java and C# is that there's a lot less abstraction between the raw muscle of the string in C++ than in other languages. It's important that you understand the underlying concepts of arrays and pointers before you jump into the more developed and abstract parts of the language. There are lots of useful tools in C++, strings included, but they take a higher level understanding of the language to really grasp and use effectively. Otherwise, you could end up with compilation errors or other problems that simply make no sense at all.

Let's look at a string conceptually. We spoke earlier about arrays. A string is simply an abstracted character array. In fact, in C, that's precisely what they were. Strings were once programmed as character arrays, like such:

```
char[] str = "hello";
```

But this is deprecated and also rather difficult to work with, and a pain even when you do know how to work with them. The new C++ standards offer a far superior manner of handling strings.

The first thing you'll want to do to work with these templates is import a library called "string". The header of your file would look like this:

```
#include <iostream>
#include <string>
```

The strings you handle from hereon are classes from the string template, which means they have a bunch of useful functions built right in.

Learning to manipulate strings is crucial to a lot of things and could prove useful in the future.

Go ahead and create a new project and call it StringManipulation. Delete the contents of main.cpp. Import <iostream> and <string> and declare your main function.

The first thing we're going to do is create a string. Let's call it x.

```
string x = "";
```

We're going to initialize it to have no value right now, as it doesn't really need one and it's not a generally good idea in terms of memory and resource management to leave uninitialized variables and objects lying around.

Before we manipulate the input, let's allow the user to enter the value of our string. However, we can't do this by using the standard console input stream. If we try to do this, then it's going to cut off after the first space, because the input stream sees this as the start of a new argument/variable.

Instead, we have to use the std namespace method "getline()", which takes the arguments of the current input stream as well as the string which is going to assume the value of the line that was received.

```
getline(cin, x);
```

Now that we've got the string, we're going to do some things with it.

First, let's print out a substring from the second character to the second to last character.

The string class has some handy built-in functions for things like this.

The function for substring is *string name*.substr(), and it accepts the arguments of the beginning index and the end index.

Remember how we talked earlier about how strings were just character arrays? Well, let's say that the user entered "cat" as the string.

This would be interpreted, ultimately, as a four character array which goes like this:

0	1	2	3
c	a	t	\0

Where \0 is the null termination escape character which denotes the end of a string. If you had manually entered the string, like:

```
string x = "cool";
```

then it wouldn't be there. However, since we got the line, it's there per necessity.

So the index of the second character of the string would be 1, of course. But since the user can input strings of various lengths, we need to get ahold of the string length somehow to get the second to last character.

There's a function for that, thankfully. The *string*.length() function helps you to find the length of a string. To find the second to last character, we first have to subtract the last technical character of the string - the null termination character - and then the last real character of the phrase. The substring method should thus look like this:

```
x.substr(1, x.length() - 2)
```

You can output this, like anything else, straight to the console output stream. Your line should look something like this:

```
cout << "Substring: " << x.substr(1,
x.length() - 2) << "\n";
```

The string library is chock full of useful functions that you very well could end up using in the future. For example, in addition to creating substrings, you can also append things to a string and insert characters into the middle of them.

Chapter 10: STL/C++ Standard Library: Containers, Algorithms, Iterators

A common misnomer is to refer to the C++ Standard Library as the STL. The STL, or Standard Template Library, was a standard developed sometime in the past. The C++ Standard Library is a set of templates, many of which were adopted from the STL. The STL is now deprecated, but some extremely useful templates remain.

Earlier, when we were creating arrays, you may have noticed one massive issue with them: you can't expand them. They have a set size and don't grow or shrink. What if there were a way to fix this?

The Standard Library offers a solution to this problem in the form of containers. Containers manage sets of data of the same type. They include vectors, sets, and lists, among others.

Vectors are much like arrays, except they handle their own storage and size.

Much like with strings, you need to import the vector library in order to use the template:

```
#include <vector>
```

Now you're able to access everything regarding vectors.

You declare a template like so:

```
template<type> variableName;
```

Let's say we wanted to go back to the earlier example of grades, creating a self-sizing array of grades. We'd declare it like this:

```
vector<int> grades;
```

Adding values to a template is simple. You had an element by using the concept of pushing and popping. You push a new value onto the vector, or you pop a value off.

Let's say the first grade you wanted to add was a 55 (poor guy.) We could do this by typing:

```
grades.push_back(55);
```

You've now added your first value to the vector.

What if you want to add a set of values? Well, luckily, in C++11 you can also insert a set of vectors in a similar manner to which you initialize a set of values in an array, using the *vector*.insert() function. This takes two arguments: the index at which you start inserting, and the values you'd like to insert. If you have multiple values in your vector, you can just use vector.end() to find the point of insertion.

```
    grades.insert(grades.end(), { 96, 64, 75,
83 });
```

In earlier versions, you would need to create a temporary array to insert the data.

```
int[] tmp = { 96, 64, 75, 83 };
grades.insert(grades.end(), tmp, tmp + 4);
```

In order to go through every item in the list, you can use something called a for each loop in other languages. If we wanted to print out every item on the list, we would do the following:

```
for (int i : grades) {
    cout << i << "\n";
}
```

What if we weren't using a primitive data type but instead an object? There's support for that as well, using something called iterators. By the usage of iterators, you can access methods of the object (such as .length() or .substr() for a string).

If we had a vector of strings, for example, called *j* and we wanted to print the length of every string therein:

```
for (string i : j) {
                cout << i << " - string length:
" << i.length() << "\n";
    }
```

You can do this for any object you create, but we'll talk more explicitly about that when we actually start creating objects in the next chapter.

Another type of container, lists, functions very similarly to vectors. The specific differences between these two are beyond the grasp of a relative beginner, but the general rule concerning these two types of containers is that vector is generally the one that should be used, *unless* you have to constantly add or erase elements from anywhere other than the end of the container.

There's another type of container called an associative container, which is formatted with a key value and a mapped value. It's generally ordered according to the keys. The most prominent type of associative container is called a map. This is great when you need to associate a set of data by a certain trait. For a real world example, a store's inventory system could be kept with a map of SKU codes (integers - the key) and item names (strings - the mapped data).

For this, you'd import <map>, and declare a map by:

```
map<int, string> Inventory;

Inventory[00400030] = "Tamagotchi, blue";
Inventory[00400031] = "Tamagotchi, white";
Inventory[00324359] = "Twilight, DVD";
Inventory[44539294] = "Dark Souls, Xbox
360";
```

If you wanted to recall a specific element later in your code, you could do something along the lines of:

```
cout << "Inventory[00400030] is: " <<
Inventory[00400030] << "\n";
```

Calling Inventory[00400030] would print out the mapped value, here being "Tamagotchi, blue".

There's another type of associative container called a set. Sets function very similar to maps, except that they don't allow duplicates. Maps allow duplicate values, but not duplicate keys.

Also included in the STL is a library called "algorithms". This library can be used in order to search, sort, and manipulate element ranges.

Included in these are functions such as equal(), which determines if two sets of elements are equal to each other. There's also transform(), which applies a given function to a given range.

Chapter 11: File I/O

There will often be times where you'll need to read or write from files. C++ has a large amount of functionality for this very sort of thing by way of the <fstream> header.

The primary way of utilizing this class is to use the two main variables ofstream and ifstream, meaning output file stream and input file stream.

Create a new project called FileIO and delete the contents of main.cpp.

Set it up like normal but below iostream, include additionally fstream and string.

In your main function, declare an instance of ofstream called "file1" and a string called "input".

In order to read or write files, we have to open them. To do this, below the variable declaration, we need to type the following:

```
file1.open("cool.txt");
```

Now to write to this file, consider the following: *cout* is an output stream, correct? You write into this using the output stream operator (<<). You treat your file the same way, as it's simply an output stream. To write to this file, you'd simply write:

```
file1 << text here
```

So let's allow the user to write to this file until they type "EXIT".

Create a while loop with the run condition that it will run for as long as the string doesn't say "EXIT".

Within the while loop, write to the fstream, getting the lines as we did earlier.

Then afterward, we need to close the file. Do so with `file1.close("cool.txt")`.

By the end, your code should look a tad like this.

```
int main() {
        ofstream file1;
        string input;

        file1.open("cool.txt");

        while (input!="EXIT") {
                getline(cin, input);

            if (input!="EXIT")
                        file1 << input <<
"\n";
        }

        file1.close();
    }
```

Reading from files is similar. Instead of ofstream, you would use ifstream.

Create a text file with digits divided by line breaks called digits.txt wherever your Codeblocks project files are, then get rid of the code you have in your main.cpp file.

Include iostream, string, and fstream again, then create your main function. Don't forget to include using namespace std in your file - it can be tricky to remember, at first!

Declare ifstream file1, a string called input, and an int called total with the value of 0.

Open your file you just created:

```
file1.open("digits.txt");
```

While this file still has lines to read, we want to do two things:
- cast the line to a string and print it out, and
- cast that string to an int, which we add to total

We do this by doing the following:

```
while (getline(file1, input)) {
    cout << input << "\n";
    total += stoi(input);
}
```

stoi() is a C++11 function which allows you to cast a string to an int, comparable to Java's Integer.parseInt() function.

We then close the file:

```
file1.close();
```

and print out the total.

By the end, your code should look like this:

```
int main() {
    ifstream file1;
    string input;
    int total = 0;

    file1.open("digits.txt");

    while (getline(file1, input)) {
        cout << input << "\n";
        total += stoi(input);
    }

    file1.close();

    cout << "The total of these is: " << total;
}
```

C++ surprisingly makes file input and output very, very simple.

Chapter 12: Introduction to Classes

At the heart of all object-oriented programming lies the notion of classes, objects that you create and utilize all throughout your code. This helps with modularity, with ease of use, with efficiency, and with higher-level programming that is far more logical and coherent.

In the early iterations of C, there was a primitive sort of class called a struct. Structs still exist in C++ but are mainly deprecated and shirked in favor of using classes instead. Nevertheless, structs are important to cover. C++ structs are also different from C structs. C structs didn't have much of the functionality which C++ structs do.

Before we jump into that, let's talk briefly about the notion of access modifiers.

We've talked about things like *int*, *string*, *bool*, and *float*, called types. We created what could be considered somewhat of a type using enumerators. However, you can actually create an entire type that is made up of smaller pieces of data and innate functions. This is called an object.

Access modifiers describe what is able to change what within your code. There are three different access modifiers.

Public access means that the object and/or its internal data and functions can be accessed and modified by any other code in the program.

Protected means that the object and/or its internal data and functions can be access and modified by only its derivatives. (This will make sense when we get into inheritance and polymorphism.)

Private means that only the object itself can access and modify its data.

This is important for purposes of security, clarity, and code safety.

Structs and classes are both ways to create new objects. The primary difference between structs is that structs are public by default and classes are private by default. Other than that, the differences are very negligible.

However, in the tech industry, structs have a fair bit of a negative connotation. Developers tend to see them as unprotected objects with little functionality, while they tend to see classes as very functional objects with child classes that are well made and well structured.

As such, it's generally better to create classes unless your object has very little in the way of functionality and simply contains very little data and innate function.

Look at this struct and declaration.

```
struct animal {
     enum diet { herbivore, omnivore,
carnivore };
     int legs;
     string name;
     diet naturalDiet;
};

int main() {
     animal dog;
     dog.legs = 4;
     dog.name = "Dog";
     dog.naturalDiet = dog.carnivore;
}
```

This is the absolutely most simple way to declare a new object. You should absolutely not declare them within an existent function.

For this chapter and the next, we're going to be talking a lot about animals, using them as an explanation for concepts because the hierarchy of the animal kingdom fits the concepts underlying classes and object-oriented programming pretty perfectly.

Let's go ahead and replace that struct with a class, because we're going to be using classes going forward as they're generally a safer and better option than structs are.

Create a new project in CodeBlocks called "AnimalSimulator". Not the most creative title, but it'll absolutely work for what we've got to do. Redact the contents of main.cpp and import iostream and create your main method.

Above the main method, let's declare a class called Animal. You would do that very similarly to how you'd declare a struct. For the sake of illustration, make it look like this:

```
class animal {
      string name;
};
```

Then within your main method, declare an instance and set its instance of name to the name of your favorite animal. Afterward, try to build.

You should have gotten an error that said "error: string animal::name is private".

Perfect. This is absolutely supposed to happen, because now we have to fix this. This is where that whole notion of access description comes in.
Modify your class so that it looks like this:

```
class animal {
      public:
            string name;
}
```

Then try to build. It should work fine this time. That's because we made the string "name" public, which means other methods/functions outside of the class itself can access it.

This is generally considered bad practice though, so we're going to rewrite the class like so:

```
class animal {
      private:
            string name;
}
```

The best-practice way to modify values within a class is to use get/set methods. Here's the way the class would look if you implemented get/set methods.

```
class animal {
      private:
            string name;

      public:
            string getName() {
                  return this->name;
            }

            void setName(string name) {
                  this->name = name;
            }
}
```

Now, in your main method, after declaring whatever animal it is, instead of directly modifying its name, you should instead use the get/set method like so (assuming your instance animal is called "dog"):

```
dog.setName("dog");
```

Then you can test this by printing out the name in your main method:

```
     cout << "The name of my favorite animal
is: " << dog.getName() << "\n";
```

The way these work is by returning or setting the value of the variable via a method from within the class. "this->" is called the **this pointer**, and it refers to the variable of a given instance of a class. Every object has access to its own variables and can modify them directly via the 'this pointer'.

Anyway, your code should work stunningly. But what if you don't want to go through get/set for every instance of every class? Well, you use what's called an initializer function.

Modify your class so it looks like this:

```
class animal {
      private:
            string name;

      public:
            animal(string name) {
                  this->name = name;
            }

            string getName() {
                  return this->name;
            }

            void setName(string name) {
                  this->name = name;
            }
      }
```

Now, in your main function, take out the chunk of code that says *animal x* followed by the *x.setName("name")* function. When you create an initializer function, you can set certain variables from the get-go.

For example, since your initializer function takes the argument of *name*, you can declare that when you declare the variable and circumvent the whole setName operation. Look at this code for an example:

```
animal dog("dog");
animal elephant("elephant");
animal bird("bird");
```

These are all separate instances of the class animal, and their names have been set without the use of a set function thanks to the function initializer.

This can take as many arguments as you'd like it to. This makes it incredibly easy to create new objects and pretty streamlined of a process too.

Now that we've spoken for a moment about declaring objects and things of that nature, let's talk more about the specifics of what you can do with them. The object *animal* here, represents, of course, animals. We can give the entire class a set of methods that they can perform.

Let's think for a second about what every animal does. Every animal sleeps, eats, and drinks, right? So it wouldn't be very outlandish to include these within our class so that every member object of the class animal is able to perform these methods.

Let's say we had two specific kinds of food: meat, and plants, both of which also represented by their own respective objects.

We could create two different functions for this:

```
void eat(plant p) {
      // code here
}

void eat(meat m) {
      // code here
}
```

Even though these share a name, you can call either depending upon the type of object which you put include in the function call, and both will perform their respective code in response to the argument which you included. This is called **function overloading**. It's an essential technique in object-oriented programming that will help you to create functional and clear sets of code that are easy for people to use and understand. In the next chapter, we're going to start exploring some of the deeper things that you can do with classes, including the inherent qualities which make them both incredibly useful and incredibly practical in object-oriented programming.

Because it's unwieldy to create a large number of types while we're learning about classes in the first place, let's just leave "eat" as a void function which doesn't take arguments. Your code should look like this:

```
class animal {
        private:
                string name;

        public:
                animal(string name) {
                        this->name = name;
                }

                string getName() {
                        return this->name;
                }

                void setName(string name) {
                        this->name = name;
                }

                void eat() {
                        // eat food
                }
        }
```

In the next chapter, we're going to cover far more in-depth concepts regarding classes.

Chapter 13: Deeper Class Concepts

When C++ was being designed by AT&T engineer Bjarne Stroustrup as a language which would extend C, it was actually called *C with Classes* at first. Resultantly, one can make the not-so-bold assumption that C has a wealth of things which you can do with classes. This assumption would be 100% correct. Classes have several different functionalities built in that make them a joy to work with.

The first we should consider is called **inheritance**. This is a concept which allows a class to draw from a parent class. Let's go back to the animal class.

Because all dogs are animals, we can create a derivative of the animal class to represent dogs.

Let's say we took that code from earlier with the class of animal. In order to inherit it, we'd have to do the following:

```
class dog : public animal {
      // code goes here
};
```

Now, let's try to change some things around. First, above your string constructor function in the *animal* class, create a constructor which doesn't take arguments and sets this->name to a blank string.

```
animal() {
      this->name = "";
}
```

Then go back to the dog class and create a mimic constructor, but here, set this->name equal to "dog". Don't forget to make your constructor public.

```
dog() {
      this->name = "dog";
}
```

Perfect. Technically, this is exactly what I've asked you to do. However, if you try to compile that, it doesn't work. You get the heads up that "string animal::name" is private, and those can't be modified.

This means that back in our animal class code, we need to make this essential change:

```
class animal {
      private:
            string name;
[...]
```

needs to become

```
class animal {
      protected:
            string name;
[...]
```

This is because in order to access this variable from child objects, we have to set the access modifiers in the ultimate parent function for this variable to *protected*. Now, child classes can access and modify this variable, but any given function in the program otherwise cannot.

Because all dogs are animals but not all animals are dogs, we can define specific functions here that dogs will perform which other animals obviously won't.

Back in your dog class, create a function under the *public* access modifier which is called "bark".

```
public:
      void bark() {
            cout << "\nBark!\n"
      }
```

Now go to your main method and declare an instance of dog. For the sake of example, mine will be called "d". Afterward, create an instance of the animal class.

Try to access bark() from both.

```
int main() {
        dog d;
        animal a;

        dog.bark();
        animal.bark();
}
```

If you try to compile, you should get the error that "'class animal' has no member named 'bark'." Great! This is exactly what was supposed to happen. Because dog is a derived class from animal, you can define functions in it that a dog can use but something broadly defined as an animal cannot - for example, barking.

Remove a.bark(), then compile and launch. It should work perfectly.

But wait! I know what you're thinking. "There are types of dog too. And furthermore, not every dog *barks*, small dogs *yip*, genius." I'm well aware. Don't worry - we can derive classes from derived classes, too!

Below your dog class, add in a class called "smallDog" which is inherited from dog.

```
class smallDog : public dog {
        public:
        smallDog() {
                        this->name = "small dog";
        }
};
```

Now if, in our main function, we create an instance of smallDog called sd, and try to declare bark after dog d barks, we'll have two barks on the screen. But you're right - small dogs *don't* bark. How do we go about fixing this?

This is where something called **function overriding** comes into play.

To override a function, you only need to rewrite it (unless it's a virtual function, in which case it needs the override specifier.)

In class *smallDog*:

```
void bark() {
        cout << "\nYip!\n";
}
```

Now, in your code, sd.bark() should produce "yip" while d.bark() produces "bark". This is the essential nature of function overriding in C++.

Function overriding is an integral part of the object-oriented concept known as "polymorphism". What this means is that things can have different meanings depending upon the context. Inheritance and polymorphism are two key concepts of object-oriented programming.

Another important concept is the notion of abstraction. Abstraction is the idea of keeping the user-level side of programming as error-free and easy to maintain as possible, often by providing functions for performing certain actions upon variables that are protected by the classes themselves from user-level access which could inadvertently cause harm to the overall program.

One more important object-oriented concept is the idea of encapsulation, which is a mechanism of putting data and functions which use them together. Classes innately offer encapsulation. Encapsulation and abstraction go hand in hand by hiding data that could potentially cause an error, instead offering methods by which to access, utilize, and manipulate the data.

Anyway, getting off of the broader concepts, it's very important to cover the topic of virtual functions.

It's a little difficult to explain why virtual functions are important, but I'm going to try, because they very much are.

The simplest way to explain it is this: let's say you've got two classes, a base class and a derived class. We can go back to the example of animals/dogs. Animals would eat generic food, while dogs would eat - of course - dog food.

If they both had a function called "isEating()" which would output what they were eating, the animal object would output "generic food" while the dog object would output "dog food". This is fine and all for the purpose of a main function, but it falls apart if they have to go through an intermediate function.

For example, if in the main function, there were a reference to another function called "makeAnimalsEat(animal &a)", and the referenced animal a were to call .isEating(), then all objects derived from the animal class would use the animal version of the function isEating and not their own overridden versions.

At first glance, a solution appears to overload the makeAnimalsEat(animal &a) function with another function that accepts specifically the derivative class *dog*, such as makeAnimalsEat(dog &d). But think about this a little further - there are a lot of animals in the world. A whole, whole lot. Are we really going to overload this same exact function repeatedly in order to make it work for every possible derivative of the animal class? Of course not, that's absurd.

The answer instead is to make the base class's isEating() function a virtual function, like so:

```
virtual void isEating() {
    cout << "generic food";
}
```

To override this function in derived classes, you type the override keyword after the function name, like this:

```
void isEating() override {
    cout << "dog food";
}
```

which would effectively solve the problem that had existed in the first place.

The last major concept of classes to cover (at least for the scope of this book) is the notion of *operator overloading*. There's a very simple way to describe this.

Think about if you had two integers a, 5, and b, 3. The equation:

a + b

would thus come out to 8. Right? This is because they have explicit values.

However, what if we had two members of a class called cube, and this class had length, height, and width as its properties.

If you had two cube objects named a and b and then tried to add them, there's no innate meaning to it. The compiler doesn't know how or in what way to add these two objects.

Create a new project called operatorOverloading and delete the contents of main.cpp. Create your main method and then create a cube class. It should have private variables length, height, and width, and public methods which set those values

74

and return the volume (length * width * height), as well as a class constructor + an empty constructor.

Your code should end up looking a bit like this:

```
class cube {
        public:
                int getV() {
                        return length * width * height;
                }

                void setL() {
                }

                void setW() {
                }

                void setH() {
                }

                cube() {
                        this->length = 0;
                        this->width = 0;
                        this->height = 0;
                }

                cube(int length, int width, int
height) {
                        this->length = length;
                        this->width = width;
                        this->height = height;
                }

        private:
                int length, width, height;
}
```

So with that done, we now need to look at how we could add two cube objects together.

Fortunately, you can actually overload the existent mathematical operators in C++ to give them new functions for your classes.

Here's how we would do such in this case.

First, in the public section of your cube code, you would act like you were making a constructor by declaring the object itself.

```
cube
```

Then you use the operator keyword and what specify which operator you want to override - in this case, the addition operator, followed by parameter parentheses and function brackets.

```
cube operator+(cube &add) {
}
```

Since we're passing through another object, we need to actually pass in the secondary variable's reference address. What's happening in this line of code is that you're overriding the addition operator, +, and specifying what happens when the object *cube* is combined with the operator and the object within the parameters. So basically, what happens when *this* instance of cube cube is added to another cube, here called *add*? Within the brackets, we need to specify what's going on.

In the brackets, we need to declare cube c.

Now, we need to say that cube c's length is equal to the length of the first cube instance (this->) plus the second cube instance defined in the function parameters (add).

```
c.length = this->length + add.length;
```

Then we do the same for the width and height.

By the end, your code should ideally look something along these lines:

```
cube operator+(cube &add) {
    cube c;
    c.length = this->length + add.length;
    c.width = this->width + add.width;
    c.height = this->height + add.height;
    return c;
}
```

If you wanted your code to be extra secure, you could actually make the variable within the parameters a constant.

```
cube operator+(const cube &add) {
```

Now we're going to talk about splitting your code up to make it incredibly readable and easier to use.

Chapter 14: Modularity in C++ via Namespaces and Headers/Preprocessor Directives/Other .cpp Files

Modularity is the property of something being broken down into crucial parts. We're just going to jump straight into this lesson and avoid any time-wasting here.

Occasionally, in C++, you'll run into a conflict where you have two imported modules or two classes that share a name. Namespaces help you to avoid this problem.

Namespaces are generally defined like so:

```
namespace gradebook {
    class Student {
        // code here
    public:
        void addAssignment(const
Assignment &a) {
            // add assignment to vector
        }
    }

    class Assignment {
        // code here
    }

    void listStudents() {
        // code here
    }
}
```

In order to access these classes from elsewhere in your code, you'd have to do something along the lines of:

```
int main() {
    gradebook::Student student;
    gradebook::Assignment assignment;

    student.addAssignment(assignment);

    gradebook::listStudents();
}
```

with "gradebook::" being the way to access members of the gradebook namespace. You can, however, circumvent this by adding "using namespace gradebook" to your code, preferably below "using namespace std". While we're at it, you don't even necessarily have to include "using namespace std" in your code. Since it *is* a namespace, you can technically access everything within it by using the namespace directive:

```
std::string out= "Hello world!";
std::cout << out;
```

Often, namespaces will be defined within header files. This helps the idea of modularity by promoting the idea of using existing modules and creating new ones that make code quicker to use in the future.

Header files are files which contain large chunks of code definitions that can be used in other code. For example, a header file could technically have an add function which took two variables and returned the sum. You could include this header file in your main.cpp and then have access to said function.

In order to create a header file, you have to define it with something called preprocessor directives.

Now's a better time than any to get into exactly what preprocessor directives are.

All C++ code has to be compiled. Preprocessor directives tell the preprocessor to look at something before the code is compiled and then does something to impact the code or program in one way or another.

There are several different kinds of preprocessor directives.

Firstly there are macro definitions, such as #define and #undef. These allow you define something used in your text to be replaced by something else during compilation. For example:

```
#define INCH_PER_FOOT 12

int main() {
        cout << "In 7 feet, there are " << 7
/ INCH_PER_FOOT << " inches.\n";
    }
```

It can also be used with ternary expressions to describe function macros.

The others are conditional operators. #ifdef, #ifndef, #elifdef, and so on.

To show you the usefulness of header files and extra CPP files, we're actually going to start a new project, and we're going to call this project Gradebook. (believe it or not!)

We're going to keep main.cpp this time, you have enough practice. Just redact the hello world portion.

Since this is our first time using multiple files for one project, I'm going to try to keep it pretty self-explanatory. This is going to tie in a lot of concepts that we've used so far to produce some really pretty and easy to use code in our main file, while also teaching you about modularity.

C++ projects are generally broken down into two parts: the interfaces (the header files), and their implementations (the C++ files). The interfaces are meant to be reusable and extensible. For the purpose of this project, we're going to make a gradebook, store our class data within a namespace in the header file, store important functions in other C++ files, and use our header file to declare those so that our main file can be very readable and straightforward.

Anyway, for now, you're going to go to File -> New -> Empty file. Create a file called "gradebook.h". We need to throw the preprocessor some directives, so here's what we're going to do:

```
#ifndef GRADEBOOK_H
#define GRADEBOOK_H

#endif
```

Between the #define and #endif directives, we're going to create our main namespace "gradebook". Within this, we're going to create two classes: Assignment, and Student.

The assignment class should have a public field with:
- a constructor which takes a string for the assignment name and a float for the grade point

It should have a private field with:
- a string: assignmentName
- a float: grade

Student should have a public field with:
- a constructor which takes a string for the student name
- a function which adds an assignment to a vector of assignments, which takes said assignment as an argument
- a function which returns the student's name

and a private field with:
- a vector<Assignment> called grades
- a string for the student's name

82

Your code should look a bit like this:

```cpp
#include <vector>
#include <string>

#ifndef GRADEBOOK_H
#define GRADEBOOK_H

using std::vector;
using std::string;

namespace gradebook {
    class Assignment {
    public:
        Assignment(std::string name, float grade)
{

            this->assignmentName = name;
            this->grade = grade;
        }
    private:
        std::string assignmentName;
        float grade;
    };

    class Student {
    public:
        Student(std::string name) {
            this->name = name;
        }
        void addGrade(Assignment &assignment) {
            this->grades.push_back(assignment);
        };
        string getName() {
            return this->name;
        }
    private:
        std::vector<Assignment> grades;
        std::string name;
    };
}

#endif
```

We're done with the header for right now.

Go to file -> new -> empty file and name it load.cpp.

Within this file, include iostream, vector, and your header - "gradebook.h".

You're going to be using std::vector, and the Student class from the namespace we just created. Tell the compiler you're using by typing *using gradebook::student*.

Here, we want to make a function which will return nothing. Call it loadStudents, and let it take an argument of a vector of students. The idea here is that we're going to be sending in a vector from our main class and populating it with students.

Use *vector<student>*.push_back(Student(*name*)) to populate it with students.

However, what if we wanted to read in students from a file instead of hardcoding everyone?

This is where our overloading lesson comes in handy. Let's create a second function called loadStudents, which takes a vector of students but also a string called "filename". At the top of your file, include fstream, and in your load students file, make two variables: an std::ifstream variable called file, and an std::string variable called input.

Open the file, taking the argument *filename* as the filename. While there are lines left to read, use *vector<student>*.push_back(Student(input)) in order to read the students into the vector. It should look like this:

```
void loadStudents(vector<Student> &vec,
std::string &filename) {
        std::ifstream file;
        std::string input;
        file.open(filename);
            while( getline(file, input))
                vec.push_back(Student(input));
        file.close();
}
```

There we go! We now have two perfectly applicable loadStudents functions.

But wait a second, we can't use them in our main function yet.

See, the thing is that you have to do something called a forward declaration when you're using a function from another source file.

There are two ways to do this:

1) Declare it at the beginning of your main.cpp file, after your using statements but before your main function.
2) Declare it within your header file.

We're going to do the latter because it's far cleaner.

So we go into the header file and after our gradebook namespace is where we're going to want to declare these functions.

```
    void
loadStudent(vector<gradebook::Student> &vec);
    void
loadStudent(vector<gradebook::Student> &vec,
std::string &filename);
```

At this point we can go back to our main file and assure that everything is working as expected.

Firstly, create a new vector of Students called studentList.

Call the loadStudents function, giving it the argument of the vector you just created.

Run a for each loop on it:

```
for (Student s : studentList) {
    cout << s.getName << "\n";
}
```

This is a springboard for a lot of other functionality going forward.

Let's try to give the students some assignments now, they're lacking those. They've got a built-in function for that, so let's just find a student and... wait a second. It's a little difficult to find a student within a vector. We can implement two ways to correct this to make it easier on the poor little teachers that have to work their way around a console gradebook. We can list vector position by the student name and allow them to input it in order to enter grades, or we can have them enter a name and search through the vector string to see if it's in there.

The first option is more efficient on the user end, so let's do that.

Let's repurpose our for loop, or rather our cout statement.

It's now going to print out the current index alongside the student name, which will tell us where in the vector each student is. Since arrays index automatically like an array, we know that they start at 0. So we can just have an integer i, which starts at 0, and iterates up with each pass through the loop. Our cout function now should look like this:

```
cout << i << " : " << s.getname() << "\n";
```

After this, we're going to test this out. Create an int called input, then run it through cin.

Output the value of studentList.at(input).getName();

Compile and test it out. It should work great, and look a bit like this:

```cpp
#include <iostream>
#include <vector>
#include "gradebook.h"

using namespace std;
using gradebook::Student;

int main()
{
    int i = 0, input;
    vector<Student> studentList;

    loadStudents(studentList);

    for (Student s : studentList) {
        cout << i << " : " << s.getName() << "\n";
        i++;
    }

    cin >> input;

    cout << studentList.at(input).getName();

    return 0;
}
```

If all goes well, then fantastic. We know that our code works now, which is
great. Now what we need to do is change utilize what we just did in order to enter a grade. Simple enough, right?

We're going to change that cout statement to say "Enter the assignment name, and then the grade."

Then we're going to accept a line of input stored to a string called "assignmentName" and we're going to filter in a float variable called grade through cin. We're doing them both through standard input stream cin for simplicity's sake. Afterwards, we're going to use studentList.at(input).addGrade(*assignment*) in order to give that student a new grade.

A little daunting sounding, but it makes sense and will work great.

By the end of it, your code should look somewhat like this:

```
cin >> assignmentName >> grade;

    Assignment a =
Assignment(assignmentName, grade);

    studentList.at(input).addGrade(a);
```

Now we need to test it out. Let's go into the assignment class and add a way to return both the name and the grade. We also need to go into the student class and add a way to return their vector of assignments.

Your Assignment and Student classes should ideally look like this:

```cpp
class Assignment {
  public:
      Assignment(std::string &name, float grade)
{
          this->assignmentName = name;
          this->grade = grade;
      }

      string getName() {
          return assignmentName;
      }

      float getGrade() {
          return grade;
      }
  private:
      std::string assignmentName;
      float grade;
  };

  class Student {
  public:
      Student(std::string name) {
          this->name = name;
      }
      void addGrade(Assignment &assignment) {
          this->grades.push_back(assignment);
      };
      std::vector<assignment> getGrades() {
          return this->grades;
      }
      string getName() {
          return this->name;
      }
  private:
      std::vector<Assignment> grades;
      std::string name;
  };
```

Now let's put this to good use.

Start a cout function that says the student's name, then the assignment name, then the grade on said assignment.

My code ended up looking like this, your should look similar. It's very heavyweight and there are ways to make this easier on the eyes, but for our purposes, it works.

```
        cout << "The student's name is: " <<
studentList.at(input).getName() << ".\n"
            << "Their grade on assignment " <<
studentList.at(input).getGrades().at(0).getName()
            << " was " <<
studentList.at(input).getGrades().at(0).getGrade();
```

There are a lot of ways to improve upon this gradebook, but this was mainly to show you the many uses of modularity within C++ and the great usefulness of things like namespaces.

You could implement all of this code within a few loops in order to make putting in grades easier, you could even implement something similar to a menu for the program if you wanted to. There are a lot of possibilities with this. The main reasoning behind this entire chapter was to show you the immense capabilities of C++ for dividing big projects into little chunks.

Imagine if we'd had to implement all of that into one function for just a single little program? It would have been nearly a hundred and fifty lines of code for about 3 lines of input and very little computation.

With that said, it's as important to have a solid infrastructure to your program as it is with anything.

That, in fact, is the whole idea behind object-oriented programming: providing better infrastructure and better ways to utilize the code underlying the concepts.

I, myself, am a very strict adherent to this idea - arguably too much so! If something can be made into a class or made into a function, I will always try to do exactly that.

The beauty of modularity is the potential for reuse. You may define functions or algorithms within a header that can be reused over and over across several programs.

A fantastic example of this kind of modularity would be a game engine. Game engines provide for a number of important functions such as graphics, audio, receiving input from both keyboard and controller, and doing things with all of that, keeping a loop running (called the game loop, interestingly enough,) and helping you with multithreading and garbage collection (automatic memory management.)

Having to recode all of these concepts as you go from project to project would be painstaking and nearly impossible. Not to mention that a modular approach allows you to break it down when something goes wrong and fix one set of code instead of having to fix an entire x00 or x000 amount of lines.

With that lesson complete, this book is pretty much brought to a close.

Conclusion

Thank for making it through to the end of *C++: Beginner to Pro Guide*, let's hope it was informative and able to provide you with all of the tools you need to achieve your goals whatever it may be.

The next step is to apply these in your knowledge as you program. As with anything, the ultimate way to become better is through practice, practice, and more practice.

I advise seeking out open-source projects and seeing what you can break down from the source code. Think of projects that would be fun to tackle - learning to program GUIs, making a basic web browser, making a music player, writing a game engine - and then take that all step-by-step, breaking it down first to the things that you know and then building on top of that.

For example, if you were to want to build a web browser, you'd have to work with connecting to the internet for sending and receiving data, which is beyond the scope of this book. If you wanted to build a peer-to-peer chat client, you'd have to work with making direct tunnels to another computer, such that you two can have a conversation directly to each other's consoles or chatboxes.

Once you have an idea of what you want to do, search for a tutorial on how to do it - or if you want to find your own way, seek out APIs that could help you out and then look at their documentation in order to figure out how to use them.

Regardless of what you end up doing, the way to get better at anything is to push yourself and practice as hard as you possibly can to be the best that you can be at it.

This book was only the beginning. You've now mastered the fundaments of C++ programming, but there's a long road ahead, and every project is going to have its own problems and its own demands. I just hope that I've reasonably armed you well enough to deal with any issues that may crop up.

Finally, if you found this book useful, a review on Amazon is always appreciated!

Other Books by Timothy Short

SQL: Beginner to Pro Guide

Linux: The Quick Start Beginners Guide

PowerShell: Beginner to Pro Guide

Blockchain: The Comprehensive Guide to Mastering the Hidden Economy

Raspberry Pi 3: Beginner to Pro Guide

WordPress: Beginner to Pro Guide

Shopify: Beginner to Pro Guide

Passive Income: The Ultimate Guide to Financial Freedom

Project Management: Beginner to Professional Manager and Respected Leader

Evernote: Made Simple: Master Time Management and Productivity

All available via amazon.com

———